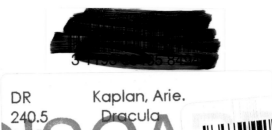

Vampires

Dracula: The Life of Vlad the Impaler

Arie Kaplan

rosen publishing's
rosen central

New York

Published in 2012 by The Rosen Publishing Group, Inc.
29 East 21st Street, New York, NY 10010

Library of Congress Cataloging-in-Publication Data

Kaplan, Arie.
Dracula: the life of Vlad the Impaler / Arie Kaplan. — 1st ed.
    p. cm. — (Vampires)
Includes bibliographical references and index.
ISBN 978-1-4488-1229-5 (library binding)
ISBN 978-1-4488-2232-4 (pbk.)
ISBN 978-1-4488-2233-1 (6-pack)
1. Vlad III, Prince of Wallachia, 1430 or 31–1476 or 7—Juvenile literature. 2. Wallachia—Kings and rulers—Biography—Juvenile literature. 3. Wallachia—History—Juvenile literature. 4. Dracula, Count (Fictitious character)—Juvenile literature. I. Title.
DR240.5.V553K37 2012
949.8'014092—dc22

[B]
                                                                    2010016161

Manufactured in Malaysia

CPSIA Compliance Information: Batch #S11YA: For further information, contact Rosen Publishing, New York, New York, at 1-800-237-9932.

On the cover: This portrait of Vlad the Impaler is located in Ambras Castle in Austria.

CONTENTS

INTRODUCTION

IN the annals of [...] above all others: Dracula! Count Dracula is [...] ultimate creature of the night, and the star of the [...]. What Superman is to superheroes, what Sherlock Holmes is to detectives, Count Dracula is to monsters. This fictional vampire was named after a real-life Romanian prince, Vlad Dracula, aka Vlad the Impaler and Vlad Tepes. He was a fifteenth-century *voivode*, or warrior prince, of the House of Basarab. Vlad Tepes was indeed bloodthirsty, although in a different way than the fictional Dracula was.

Who was the real Dracula? Like many politicians, Vlad Tepes was a complex individual. To some, he was a mass murderer. To others, he was a national hero. He tortured and killed many of his own citizens. However, he also managed to keep his beloved Walachia (now a part of present-day Romania) safe from invasion by the Ottoman Turks. So while some might say that he was a cruel and sadistic tyrant, others would argue that he was a good leader who did what was necessary to maintain order. In a way, both would be right.

Over the years, many tales have been told of Vlad Tepes's exploits. Some of these are just myths, or legends. Others are undisputed true stories. Fascinatingly enough, some of the more blood-curdling anecdotes about this all-too-human prince have been woven into the tapestry of modern-day vampire lore. When one thinks of legendary historical tyrants, one thinks of Genghis Khan, Attila the Hun, and Ivan the Terrible. Yet, none of them served as the jumping-off point for an entire branch of fiction (and, later, monster movies and TV shows). That honor was reserved for Vlad the Impaler.

THE LEGACY OF THE DRAGON

FOR the past century, every vampire story in the Western world has owed a debt to a novel published by the Irish author Bram Stoker in 1897. That novel was *Dracula*, the first book to popularize the concept of the vampire as a mysterious, immortal, romantic figure, an antihero for the ages. Bram Stoker's novel has inspired everything from the 1931 film *Dracula* starring Bela Lugosi, to British vampire movies of the 1960s starring Christopher Lee, to the 1997–2003 TV series *Buffy the Vampire Slayer*, to the recent Twilight series of novels and films. Brooding, mysterious, pale-skinned vampires like Edward Cullen of the Twilight series would not exist without Stoker's brooding, mysterious, pale-skinned Count Dracula.

Why did Bram Stoker name the main character of his novel *Dracula* after Vlad Dracula? What was it about this notorious historical figure that so fascinated him? It's possible that Stoker was simply influenced by the exotic quality of Dracula's name and his native country of Romania. When Stoker wrote *Dracula*, the

Ulrike Wyche, head of the Dracula Museum in Germany, gazes at a first-edition copy of Bram Stoker's 1897 novel, *Dracula*. Next to Wyche is a bust of actor Max Schreck, who portrayed Dracula in the 1922 silent film *Nosferatu*.

Romanian countryside was considered atmospheric, mysterious, even spooky. What a perfect place to set a vampire story!

Stoker took certain aspects from the real-life Dracula and layered them into his vampire tale. Both the real-life Dracula and the fictional Dracula had a relative who betrayed his own people to the Turks. And like his real-life counterpart, the vampiric Dracula was the scion of an aristocratic family who considered it their sacred duty to guard their homeland against the Ottoman Turks.

Unlike his immortal namesake, Vlad Dracula didn't live in Transylvania (although, as we'll see, he was born there). In fact, to understand where Dracula came from, it's necessary to realize that fifteenth-century Romania was a very different place than it is today. At the time, the central part of Romania was Transylvania, which was in turn connected to two independent provinces, Moldavia and Walachia. Walachia was Dracula's home, and he was fiercely protective of his native soil. To fully appreciate who Dracula was, one has to first understand a little about his family.

THE ORDER OF THE DRAGON

In the 1931 film *Dracula*, actor Bela Lugosi can be seen proudly wearing a metal cross, possibly signifying allegiance to a chivalric order of some kind. The historical Dracula's father was a member of just such an order.

Dracula's father was a Romanian prince whose given name—like that of his son—was Vlad; more specifically, he was Prince Vlad II of the House of Basarab. Vlad II was wise and just—and ambitious. In fact, the only person who could tame his ambitious nature was his more evenhanded wife, Princess Cneajna of the Musatin dynasty of Moldavia. Princess

Dracula was born in the Transylvanian town of Sighisoara, Romania, in 1431. The house he was born in, seen here, still stands to this day.

Cneajna was a devout Catholic with a love of scholarly pursuits.

In 1431, Vlad II was inducted into the Royal Order of the Dragon, a secret fraternal order created in 1387 to crusade against the Turks. The emblem for the Order of the Dragon was a dramatic one: a dragon, wings extended, hanging on a cross. The image of a dragon with its wings extended is eerily batlike in appearance. And in the novel *Dracula* (as in many other vampire stories), vampires possess the power to transform into bats. Perhaps this is what inspired Stoker to give his vampire count that specific superpower.

Dracula's father lived in and governed the town of Sighisoara, Transylvania, from 1431 to 1435. After joining the prestigious Order of the Dragon in 1431, Vlad II began seeking a way to gain the Walachian throne. This would mean expelling the then-current prince of Walachia, Alexandru Aldea, who was Vlad II's half-brother. There followed much infighting among the Basarab family, which culminated in Vlad II taking the throne of Walachia during the winter of 1436–1437.

Wanting to instill fear and respect in his enemies, Vlad II decided to forego his birth name, and he became known only as Dracul (or "the Dragon") after joining the Order of the Dragon. Vlad II chose a curious creature to use as his namesake—in fifteenth-century Europe, the dragon was a symbol of the devil. Moreover, the Romanian word *Dracul* means both "the dragon" and "the Devil." It's a safe bet that whenever superstitious Romanian peasants saw Vlad II clad in his battle armor, hoisting a standard emblazoned with the image of a dragon, they assumed he was on a first-name basis with Lucifer himself.

Oswald Von Wolkenstein (*above*) was a member of the Order of the Dragon, the same society to which Vlad II belonged. Note the chivalric cross worn by Von Wolkenstein and its similarity to the cross worn around the neck of *Dracula* actor Bela Lugosi (*right*).

It's important to note that, beginning with Bram Stoker's novel *Dracula*, devil imagery became entwined with the vampire myth. Indeed, it is implied that Stoker's Count Dracula had forsaken God and made a pact with the devil in order to gain eternal life. Perhaps, when Stoker had this in mind, he was thinking of Vlad II, who had forsaken his Christian name and preferred to be known as "the Devil."

SON OF THE DEVIL

In the Romanian language, adding the suffix "a" at the end of a name means "son of." Several months after Vlad Dracul joined the Order of the Dragon, his son Prince Vlad III was born. Vlad II was only too happy to nickname his son "Dracula," which means both "son of the Dragon" and "son of the Devil." This nickname would follow the child for the rest of his life.

Dracula was born in 1431 in the Transylvanian town of Sighisoara. In some ways, he was just like any other boy—a rough-and-tumble ball of energy who was always getting involved in some manner of mischief. But whereas most children spend their formative years playing with dolls and toys, Dracula played with swords and shields, as did his brothers Mircea and Radu. Vlad II decided early on that no "son of the Dragon" was going to be raised as anything but a warrior-in-training. With this in mind, he fitted his progeny with child-sized suits of armor and taught them everything from horseback riding to fencing.

Dracula and Mircea strongly resembled their father, in both looks and temperament. Like him, they were strong-willed and energetic, and they took to the study of warfare with unabashed glee. Radu, however, was soft-spoken and good-looking—as an adult, he would be known as "Radu

THE DRACULA LEGEND IS BORN

The fact that Prince Vlad III was known by so many different nick-names confused scholars and historians for centuries. Stories about Dracula circulated in various parts of the world, such as Germany, Greece, Hungary, Romania, and Turkey. Some tales told of the fearsome Dracula, Son of the Devil. Other legends told of Dracula, Son of the Dragon. Still other legends focused on Dracula the Impaler. As a result, a Byzantine historian reading about the heroic Dracula fighting against the Turks might not have realized that he was reading the same story as a German scholar studying the Son of the Devil and his horrific exploits. Only recently have Romanian scholars pieced together these diverse tales, and in doing so, they've managed to reveal the fascinating mosaic that is Dracula's life story.

the Handsome." Radu gravitated to his mother, Cneajna, who schooled the boys in the arts and humanities. It was noteworthy that Radu and Dracula didn't see eye to eye as children: later in life, they would become bitter rivals. However, at this point they were just ordinary siblings. And, although they did not know it, their lives were about to become a lot more interesting.

DRACULA COMES OF AGE

IN Bram Stoker's novel *Dracula*, the title character is descended from a family that was constantly at war with the Ottoman Turks. This backstory was most likely informed by the life of the real Dracula, who was also the latest in a long line of champions defending their kingdom against the Turks. In fact, this constant feud would profoundly inform the early years of Dracula's life.

THE DRAGON AND THE SULTAN

When Dracula was a young boy, his father sat on the throne in Targoviste, the capital of Walachia. Vlad II was a fair and just ruler. However, in some ways, he wasn't *really* the ruler of Walachia. Instead, the Turkish sultan Murad II was the true power behind the throne. This was the result of an agreement that Vlad made with Sultan Murad. The Dragon, noticing that the Turks were gaining in power, allied himself with Murad. As a result of this alliance, Murad's soldiers could come and go

Murad II was the sultan of the Ottoman Turks from 1421 to 1451. Murad held Dracula and his brother Radu captive in Adrianople, Turkey, when the siblings were children.

as they pleased, and they even had free reign to ransack Walachia. Worst of all, in 1438, the Dragon, who considered himself a Transylvanian, was made to accompany Murad on a raid of Transylvania. In effect, the Dragon was forced to attack his own people.

The sultan's raids often included murder and looting. The mayor of the Transylvanian town of Sebes surrendered specifically to the Dragon, hoping that, as a fellow Transylvanian, he would show the townspeople mercy. The Dragon spared the citizenry of Sebes from the sultan's rampant destruction. This was an isolated incident, however. The Dragon generally carried out the sultan's orders unquestioningly, and he chafed at his own lack of power. Indeed, not only was the Dragon virtually a puppet ruler, but by entering into an accord with Sultan Murad II of Turkey, Vlad II had violated his longstanding pledge to the Order of the Dragon.

GUARDED GUESTS

Events such as the incident at Sebes also caused the sultan to question the Dragon's devotion to Turkey. Therefore, in 1442 Murad captured the Dragon and two of his sons, Dracula and Radu (then aged eleven and seven, respectively). Crossing the Danube River on their way to a personal meeting with the sultan, the three royals were bound in iron chains and brought before Murad's throne. As a test of his loyalty, the Dragon was forced to give his sons Dracula and Radu to the sultan as collateral. For the time being, the boys were prisoners of Turkey.

Although the boys were kept under constant surveillance, they were free to roam the city of Adrianople and were even allowed to court Turkish girls. Radu came to enjoy life in Turkey and fully assimilated into Turkish society.

THE ORDER OF THE DRAGON

One of the main purposes of the Order of the Dragon was to spearhead a crusade against the Ottoman Turks, who had invaded most of the Balkan peninsula. The order, cofounded by the Holy Roman Emperor Sigismund of Luxembourg, was also intent on protecting the Catholic Church against so-called heretics, or nonbelievers. And the order most definitely considered the Turks to be heretics.

The Ottoman Turks were a subdivision of the Muslim religious community that dominated the aristocracy of the Ottoman Empire. The Ottoman Empire lasted from the late thirteenth century until the early 1920s. By the time of the Dragon's reign, the Ottoman Turks were threatening to penetrate Emperor Sigismund's dominion, the Holy Roman Empire. The Dragon needed to choose which side he was on. The question was, would he choose wisely?

Dracula, however, proved to be a hostile "guest" and was sometimes whipped by the Turkish guards for his stubbornness.

THE WHITE KNIGHT

In 1444, a brave Hungarian-born prince of Transylvania, John Hunyadi, also known as the White Knight, decided to wage an ambitious crusade against the Ottoman Turks. He called upon the Dragon for help. The Dragon wanted to say yes, but he knew that if he did, the sultan's revenge would be swift. Neither Dracula nor Radu would be safe. The Dragon declined to aid the White Knight.

Hunyadi's crusade, known as the Varna Campaign, was an enormous disaster. Many were killed, including the king of Poland, Ladislas III. Hunyadi only made it out alive because the Walachians helped him to escape. Afterward, both the Dragon and his eldest son, Mircea, personally blamed Hunyadi for this disaster. At a subsequent war council, Hunyadi was pronounced responsible for the crushing defeat of the Christian warriors at Varna. Thanks largely to Mircea's testimony, Hunyadi was sentenced to death. Only his sterling reputation as the White Knight of Christendom spared his life. From that point on, Hunyadi bore a grudge against the Dragon and his family, especially Mircea, who would bear the full brunt of Hunyadi's wrath in years to come.

The following year, in 1445, Hunyadi launched a second crusade against the Ottoman Turks. This time, the Dragon rallied to his side, offering up four thousand of his own cavalrymen. This placed the Dragon in an awkward

This statue of John Hunyadi, the White Knight, stands in Budapest, Hungary. After spending many years fighting the Ottoman Turks, Hunyadi died of the plague in 1456.

position, since his children were still prisoners of the sultan. To prove his loyalty, the Dragon himself didn't spearhead the assault, instead choosing his brave son Mircea to lead the charge in his stead. The sultan, outraged by the Dragon's defiance, tortured Dracula and Radu in his dungeon.

While sitting in his cell, waiting for the sultan's men to torment him further, Dracula would often look out his window and see Turkish soldiers impaling enemy troops on stakes. The practice of impalement was relatively common in those days, and it was a particularly gruesome way to die. Victims were run through—often from one end of their body to the other—with a large sharpened stake. Witnessing this horrendous act performed over and over no doubt had its effects on young Dracula's mind. Sitting in his prison cell, he began plotting and preparing for the day when he would have his revenge on the Turks.

THE DRAGON FALLS

Meanwhile, Hunyadi and Mircea fought a losing battle against the Turks. Hunyadi's men were slaughtered. By 1447, when the battle was over, Hunyadi did something surprising: as soon as he parted ways from Mircea, the White Knight attacked the Dragon's palace. There were many reasons for this assault. The Dragon's attempts to appease the Turks had angered Hunyadi, even though Hunyadi knew that the Walachian prince had only agreed to pro-Turkish policies to save the lives of his children.

Hunyadi had never forgotten the shoddy treatment he'd endured at the hands of both the Dragon and Mircea in the aftermath of the Varna Campaign. The White Knight had lost face during his two recent campaigns, and he wanted to regain his status as a fearsome warrior by

Die walachey

This fifteenth-century illustration shows a walled city in Walachia. As an adult, Dracula ruled his subjects in Walachia with an iron fist.

conquering Walachia. If it was fear and respect the White Knight craved, he certainly earned it. Hunyadi took no chances; he had many boyars (Romanian landowners) in his pocket, and they slaughtered both the Dragon and Cneajna. Hunyadi saved the cruelest fate for Mircea, who was blinded before being buried alive.

CRUELTY IN THE FAMILY

Family infighting was quite common among royalty in the 1400s. After John Hunyadi engineered the murder of the Dragon in December 1447, he placed one of the Dragon's rivals, Vladislav II of the Danesti family, on the Walachian throne. Vladislav II and the Dragon were distant relatives, as the Danesti family could be traced back to Prince Dan, one of the Dragon's ancestors. Vladislav II had a very brief reign, ruling from late 1447 until 1448. He was deposed by Dracula, who was also a distant relation. In those days, family ties were no guarantee of preferential treatment.

PUPPET OF THE SULTAN

So, by late 1447, Dracula found himself an orphan with only one living sibling. Sultan Murad, feeling sorry for his young charge, released him from captivity and offered him a command position. Dracula agreed, but only if the sultan would make a deal with him. Under the terms of the deal, Dracula would take the throne of Walachia, usurping its then-current ruler, Vladislav II. Vladislav was merely a "puppet ruler" for Hunyadi. At the time, Vladislav and Hunyadi were both off on a crusade and were therefore distracted, making it relatively simple for Dracula to make a grab for

power. As prince of Walachia, Dracula would essentially be as much of a puppet for Sultan Murad as Vladislav was for John Hunyadi. The Turks would, in effect, have free reign of Walachia.

This deal made Murad very happy. He was impressed by Dracula's bravery and fearlessness. Besides, Murad reasoned, Vladislav would have never been loyal to the Turks, since he was clearly devoted to Hungary. Dracula, however, seemed to be loyal to whoever would help him gain the throne.

What did Dracula gain from this deal? At first, not very much. Dracula seemed at this point to be just another puppet. However, that would soon change, and the world would realize that it was unwise to cross the great and fearsome Dracula.

CHAPTER
3

EXILE AND RETURN

WHEN we think of Count Dracula and other vampires, we think of them as hunted and despised, living in the shadows. The real-life Dracula, Prince Vlad III of Walachia, began his political career this way—hiding in the shadows. Still, it wouldn't be long until he stopped hiding and emerged as a feared and respected leader of men.

THE ONCE AND FUTURE PRINCE

Dracula's first term as prince of Walachia was uneventful. For one thing, he was simply the puppet of Sultan Murad II. For another, his reign was incredibly brief, lasting only from October to November of 1448. Terrified that Hunyadi's assassins—the same assassins who murdered his father—would come for him, Dracula fled. Immediately afterward, the White Knight reinstalled his own handpicked puppet ruler, Vladislav II (whom Dracula had deposed earlier that same year),

on the throne. While Vladislav was moving back into the palace, Dracula, the once and future prince of Walachia, journeyed to Moldavia, where he was protected by his Uncle Bogdan II.

Dracula spent the next three years entrenched in his studies. His study partner in those days was Bogdan's son (and Dracula's cousin), Prince Stephen of Moldavia. The two became close friends, vowing to help and support one another. This was a vow that would pay off in later years. Sadly, these days of solitude and study were cut short when, in 1451, Bogdan was assassinated, and Dracula was a fugitive once more.

This portrait of Vladislav II and his wife is located in St. Stephen's Monastery in Meteora, Greece.

AN UNUSUAL ALLIANCE

Instead of spending the rest of his life on the run, Dracula entered into an unusual alliance with Hunyadi—the man responsible for his parents' murder. This was simply a self-preservation tactic on Dracula's part. Dracula was a good ally for Hunyadi, and the White Knight knew it.

This painting by the Italian artist Palma Giovane (1548–1628) depicts the capture of Constantinople by the Ottoman Turks in 1453.

before him. He began by putting the dragon crest emblem everywhere. It appeared on his royal stamp, on banners, and on public buildings. The dragon crest was an imposing symbol, consisting of a winged dragon embracing a cross. Now, everyone would know that Prince Vlad III was the son of the Dragon. Now, everyone would know he was Dracula.

A sign in the shape of a dragon is affixed to the front of the house in Sighisoara where Vlad Dracula was born.

FROM PRINCE TO VOIVODE

As a way to further instill fear and respect in both his subjects and his enemies, Dracula changed his royal title. Traditionally, Walachia was ruled by a *domnul*, or "prince." The domnul worked in tandem with the boyars. Dracula did away with this antiquated system, first by dubbing himself a voivode, or warrior prince. Next, he changed the rules so that the prince wasn't subservient to the boyars. Dracula did this by inviting the boyars to a sumptuous banquet. He asked them to

air their complaints about his new policies. Those who complained were brought into a courtyard, where they were immediately impaled. Two hundred boyars were impaled that day.

A VILLAIN OR A HERO?

ONE of the most fascinating things about Count Dracula, as a character, is that he is often viewed as a tragic hero, or antihero, rather than a straightforward villain. Even though he does awful things throughout the course of the novel *Dracula*, the reader feels a certain sense of pity for him. This is mainly because Bram Stoker created, in Dracula, a complex, fleshed-out character. Even though Count Dracula is the antagonist, the audience relates to him. The real-life Dracula was a similarly complex character. It's difficult to assign him an easy label, such as "hero" or "villain." In truth, he was a little of both.

VLAD THE IMPALER

Dracula governed Walachia from 1456 to 1462. Even at the time, his rule was dubbed a reign of terror. He was not shy about resorting to murder to achieve his goals. While Dracula usually killed for political reasons—to silence a spy or a traitor—he sometimes inflicted pain

Dracula's cruelty was legendary. This illustration shows the notoriously bloodthirsty tyrant calmly eating dinner outside his castle while surrounded by his enemies' impaled bodies.

OUTNUMBERED, BUT NOT OUTSMARTED

In 1462, an army of 250,000 Turks crossed the Danube River into Walachia. They may have outnumbered Dracula's mere thirty-thousand soldiers, but the cunning prince outsmarted them by employing many underhanded tactics. He poisoned their drinking water and implemented nocturnal sneak attacks, slaughtering his enemies while they slept. Much like the fictional Count Dracula, the real-life Dracula favored attacking at night.

Mainly, however, Dracula defeated his Turkish attackers by unnerving them psychologically, using a ploy that no one could have been prepared for. As the Turkish army neared Targoviste, Dracula needed to think quickly so that he could repel the attack. He had his men surround the town with the bodies of thousands of captured, impaled Turks. When the Turkish army arrived and saw their own men impaled on wooden pikes, their bodies twisting in the wind, they were so disturbed that they turned tail and fled.

In Stoker's novel, Count Dracula speaks of an ancestor who "sold his people to the Turks." The real-life Dracula also had a relative who sold out his own family to the Turks. This was his brother Radu. From his childhood tenure as a "guarded guest" among the Ottoman Turks, he had come to love and admire Turkish culture, and he now found himself an officer in the Turkish army. Radu had made a deal with the boyars of Walachia to be installed on the throne, ousting his brother.

DRACULA THE FUGITIVE

Dracula's second reign as prince of Walachia ended in the fall of 1462. Together, the boyars and Turks attacked the city of Targoviste, where

Dracula's palace was located. We don't know the exact specifics of what happened during that siege, but we do know the most famous local legend concerning that event, which involves Dracula's first wife.

According to this oft-told tale, during the siege, Dracula was stationed at his mountain retreat, accompanied by a few loyal soldiers and followers. They had gathered together to plan their next step against a small band of Turks who were in hot pursuit. However, most of the Turkish soldiers had already begun bombarding Dracula's castle at Targoviste. His wife was home in the palace. A Romanian slave in the Turkish army sent a warning to Dracula's castle, apprising him of the siege. He didn't know that Dracula wasn't home at the time. Dracula's wife retrieved the message. Not wanting to be taken into Turkish captivity for fear of what might await her as a prisoner,

Vlad the Impaler's palace was located in Targoviste, Romania. It is believed that his wife jumped from a palace window to avoid being taken prisoner.

she panicked and jumped out the palace window into the river below. She died instantly. Today, that body of water is known as Riul Doamnei, which means "the Princess's River."

After learning about his wife's death, Dracula fled, accompanied by a tiny band of mercenaries. One legend tells us that during Dracula's time as a fugitive, he found shelter in an abandoned castle near Borgo Pass, a famous location to any Dracula fan. (In Bram Stoker's novel, Count Dracula's castle is located on Borgo Pass.) After weighing his options, Dracula sought asylum with John Hunyadi's son King Matthias Corvinus of Hungary.

Once there, Dracula talked King Matthias into banding together with him. Together, Dracula announced, they could take control of Walachia back from the Turks—and more importantly, from Radu, who now sat on the throne. King Matthias agreed and provided Dracula with a small group of Slovaks and Hungarians, all of whom were supposed to lead the way for a larger Hungarian force to accompany Dracula back into Walachia.

This was a trap, however. Once Dracula began to make his way back to his homeland, he was captured under secret instructions from King Matthias, who had him arrested.

IMPRISONED IN HUNGARY

Since Dracula had recently been hailed as a great hero by various European representatives—including no less than the pope—his arrest by King Matthias was quite controversial. Many in Rome and Venice considered Dracula a heroic crusader against the Turks, and they demanded an explanation from Matthias. When questioned, Matthias presented three letters written by Dracula, in which he declared his allegiance to Sultan Mehmed and the Turks.

VLAD TEPES AT THE MOVIES

Elements of Vlad Tepes's life have found their way into various movies. For example, the tragic death of Vlad's first wife formed the basis for the opening scene of Francis Ford Coppola's 1992 film *Bram Stoker's Dracula*. The film opens with Dracula, played by Gary Oldman, returning from fighting the Turks. He finds that his wife has fallen to her death rather than surrender to Turkish invaders. The scene, not found in Stoker's novel, was invented by the filmmakers and is clearly an homage to the fate of the historical Dracula's wife. Similarly, Hungarian king Matthias Corvinus served as the inspiration for a character in a recent series of vampire films. In the *Underworld* movie franchise, Markus Corvinus is the name of the world's first vampire. And like Matthias, the fictional Markus is also the son of a Hungarian warlord.

Actor Gary Oldman was made up to resemble Vlad the Impaler in the 1992 film *Bram Stoker's Dracula*.

Historians believe that Dracula's stay at Solomon's Tower in Visegrad may have lasted roughly from 1462 to 1466. He served out the rest of his twelve years of captivity in relative freedom, although he remained exiled in Hungary. Dracula's prison term was cut short because he converted from the Orthodox faith to Roman Catholicism and remarried, this time to a relative of King Matthias.

LIFE IN HUNGARY

From what can be pieced together from the scant records that survive this period, Dracula may have wed Ilona Szilagy, Matthias's cousin. This marriage benefited Dracula in many ways. For one thing, by marrying into the Hungarian royal family, he could repair his blemished reputation. Dracula could

Solomon's Tower is located in the town of Visegrad, Hungary. Vlad Tepes is thought to have been held in the tower for about four years.

THE TORTURER OF VERMIN

According to a popular story, Dracula was said to have tortured and impaled spiders, birds, and mice and displayed them in the window of his prison cell in Visegrad. A later story, put forth by his enemies, reports that Dracula "drank the blood of his animal victims."

These stories are widely believed to be untrue. However, it's worth noting that Dracula's behavior in these anecdotes mirrors that of the character Renfield in Bram Stoker's novel *Dracula*. In the novel, Renfield is Count Dracula's servant. He is crazed and half-starved, feasting on vermin and displaying their corpses on his windowsill. It's possible that Stoker used this very real anti-Dracula propaganda to shape the fictional character of Renfield, a torturer and devourer of defenseless vermin.

also leave the confines of his prison, and King Matthias named him his official candidate to the Walachian throne. Dracula was given the rank of captain in the crusading Catholic army. This enabled him to resume his true purpose: to reestablish himself as the prince of Walachia and lead the charge against the Ottoman Turks. To that end, he would plot, plan, and bide his time until he could strike. First, his brother Radu would have to be removed from the throne. This would happen very soon, thanks to Dracula's cousin Stephen the Great of Moldavia.

Often thought of as a mere pawn of the Turks, Radu the Handsome was defeated by Stephen the Great in the spring of 1473. His immediate successor was Basarab III. However, King Matthias considered Basarab completely untrustworthy, yet another reason for him to place Dracula on the throne. Dracula had proven himself a master strategist, as well as a passionate crusader. In 1475, Matthias went so far as to put his support of Dracula in writing. That year, Matthias, Stephen, and Dracula signed a contract, pledging to aid and support one another. This powerful trio formed the spine of the new anti-Turk crusade bankrolled by the new pope, Sixtus IV.

DRACULA'S LAST STAND

Basarab III ruled until November 1475. After this date, he may have still sat on the throne, but it was only in a ceremonial capacity. Throughout the spring and summer of 1476, Dracula gained more and more power and backing from the Hungarian government, and plans were made to have Dracula regain the throne. Stephen Báthory, a member of the Hungarian noble family from Transylvania, led the charge to reinstall Dracula. In mid-November, Dracula was reinvested as the prince of Walachia. Finally, he occupied the throne again. But now, at the beginning of his third term, Dracula was surrounded by enemies. Both the Saxons and Walachian boyars considered him a blood-soaked monster. Rival claimants to the throne, such as Basarab, plotted against him, as did the Turks. Whereas before Dracula was often seen as unreasonably paranoid, now he had *every* reason to be paranoid.

By December 1476, Dracula had had no time to consolidate power, nor was he able to form alliances, which might have given him some sense

This statue of Vlad the Impaler is located in downtown Bucharest, Romania. Although he was a brutal tyrant, Dracula is considered by many Romanians to be a patriot who protected his people from outside threats.

of security. Perhaps he knew that the end was near. This would explain why he didn't bring his family with him to Walachia. It also explains why, when he went into battle for what would be the last time, the only soldiers he took with him were his Moldavian guard, a mere two hundred soldiers in number.

THE DEATH OF DRACULA

No one knows exactly how Dracula died. Nor do we know who killed him. The most likely suspects include Basarab, one of his boyars, and a Turkish warrior. What is known is that he was beheaded after he was murdered. Dracula's head was then sent to Constantinople, where it was displayed as proof that the great and powerful Vlad the Impaler was no longer a threat. It is also worth noting that, in Bram Stoker's novel, Count Dracula is decapitated. In fact, in most horror movies, beheading is one surefire way to kill the dreaded vampire.

CHAPTER 6

DRACULA LIVES

ACCORDING to legend, when Dracula was decapitated, his head was impaled on a spike. For one so obsessed with impalement, this was certainly fitting. It's also appropriate that Bram Stoker's Count Dracula can be killed by being "impaled" with a stake through the heart.

One might think that the real-life Dracula's story ended with the tyrannical prince's death. This is not so. In fact, like Stoker's Dracula, his historical predecessor has gained a measure of immortality: although his physical body died that day on the battlefield in December 1476, his legend lives on, even to this day.

Dracula's influence on popular culture began with the Bram Stoker novel, first published in 1897. Moreover, in the wake of Stoker's book, various writers, cartoonists, and filmmakers have incorporated aspects of the real Vlad Tepes's life into their fictional vampire stories. There are, of course, the aforementioned references to Vlad Tepes in films like Francis Ford Coppola's *Bram Stoker's Dracula* (1992) and the more

The 1970s' Marvel Comics series *Tomb of Dracula* featured a "Marvel Universe" version of Dracula. Marvel's Dracula was a combination of Stoker's Count Dracula and the historical Vlad Tepes.

recent *Underworld* movie franchise. Yet this is just the tip of the iceberg.

COMIC BOOK DRACULA

The Marvel Comics version of Count Dracula first gained notoriety in the celebrated 1972–1979 comic book series *Tomb of Dracula*. The Marvel Comics Dracula is a unique combination of the Bram Stoker character Count Dracula and the real-life Vlad Tepes. For example, the Marvel

Dracula's full name is Vlad Tepes Dracula, and his backstory is based on that of the historical Dracula. Like the real-life Vlad Tepes, this comic book Dracula also had brothers named Radu and Mircea. Historical figures such as John Hunyadi and Sultan Murad II factor into the story as well. Up to a certain point, the biography of the Marvel Comics Dracula closely mirrors that of his real-world predecessor—until this Dracula is bitten by a vampire. After this, he is cursed to roam the earth, thirsting for human blood. It's evident that comics writers like Gardner Fox and Marv Wolfman, who worked on the 1970s' *Tomb of Dracula* comic, were familiar with the story

of Vlad the Impaler. They were also clearly Bram Stoker fans.

CINEMATIC DRACULA

During the 1970s, Dan Curtis, the creator of the vampire soap opera *Dark Shadows*, directed a made-for-TV movie called *Dracula*, starring actor Jack Palance. This 1973 offering, based on a script by the legendary novelist and screenwriter Richard Matheson, was an adaptation of Stoker's novel but also incorporated flashbacks depicting Dracula as a medieval prince. Here, the filmmakers tossed elements of Vlad Tepes's life into the more familiar Bram Stoker story, adding layers to the Dracula character.

In the 1975 documentary *In Search of Dracula*, Vlad was played by Christopher Lee, perhaps best known

Actor Christopher Lee portrayed Count Dracula in the 1958 British horror film *Dracula*, produced by Hammer Film Productions. Lee starred in six other Dracula movies, all produced by Hammer.

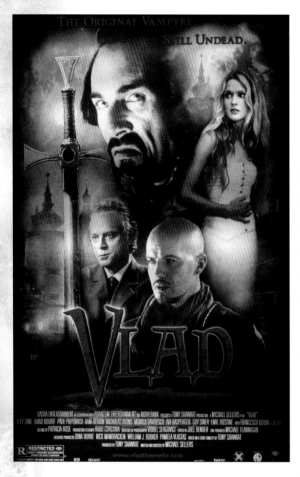

There have been a number of films about Vlad the Impaler. In the 2003 film *Vlad*, a group of American students are haunted by visions of Vlad Tepes while visiting the late tyrant's homeland.

for portraying the fictional Count Dracula in a series of British horror movies. Later, the 1979 Romanian film *Vlad Tepes* was one of the rare movies to portray Vlad the Impaler in a positive light.

More recently, the 2000 TV movie *Dark Prince: The True Story of Dracula*, directed by horror auteur Joe Chappelle, was an attempt at a serious film biography of Prince Vlad—until the end of the movie, when Vlad rises up from the grave as a vampire. In late 2009, it was even announced that Summit Entertainment, the company behind the Twilight movies, would be developing a movie called *Vlad*, a period film centering on Vlad Tepes's life as a young prince.

LEGEND BECOMES MYTH

All of this fascination with Dracula's legacy raises the question: how is Dracula remembered today in his native land of Romania? Surprisingly enough, he's considered a hero in much of his homeland. Over the course

THE FICTIONAL DRACULA MEETS THE REAL DRACULA

Not only have many films, TV shows, and comic books made Vlad Dracula and Count Dracula one and the same, but no less than Bram Stoker himself suggests that very notion in his famous novel! It's a fleeting, blink-and-you'll-miss-it moment, but it's there nonetheless. At one point in the book, famed vampire hunter Abraham Van Helsing says of the count: "He must, indeed, have been that Voivode Dracula who won his name against the Turk, over the great river on the very frontier of Turkey-land." What other Voivode Dracula could Stoker have been talking about, since *voivode* is Romanian for "warrior prince"? And what other real-life Romanian warrior prince, named Dracula, was notorious for fighting against the Turks? Here, the Van Helsing character is implying that at some point, perhaps Vlad Tepes may have become an actual vampire!

of the past few centuries, Dracula's heroic qualities have been emphasized, and his cruel acts downplayed. The Dracula folktales passed down orally by generations of Romanian peasants (Romanian didn't exist as a written language until the sixteenth century) portrayed Vlad III as a righteous citizen, obsessed with upholding the law and punishing the wicked. When viewed in a certain light, this makes sense. Because of Dracula's strong stance against boyars—who were seen as the privileged upper class—he seems like a Robin Hood of Romania, someone who robbed the rich to give to the poor. His hatred of the Turks was seen as patriotism. Finally, his crimes against his own people were often justified as simply doing away with "undesirables" during wartime, when rulers must make tough choices.

What does all this mean? Does it excuse the awful things that Dracula did? Of course not. However, it does illustrate how history can become legend and how legend can become myth. Vlad's story also shows how the exploits of one real monster can ignite the popular imagination, giving rise to generations of fictional monsters.

1387

The Order of the Dragon is founded.

1431

Prince Vlad II of the House of Basarab is inducted into the Order of the Dragon. That winter, Prince Vlad III is born in Sighisoara, Transylvania. His father nicknames the boy Dracula.

1436-1437

The Dragon overtakes the throne of Walachia. Dracula considers Walachia his home from this point on.

1442

Murad II, sultan of the Ottoman Turks, holds Dracula and his brother Radu as prisoners in Adrianople.

1444

John Hunyadi wages a crusade against the Ottoman Turks. The Dragon declines to help him. Hunyadi's crusade, known as the Varna Campaign, is a dismal failure.

1445

Hunyadi launches a second crusade. This time, the Dragon helps out, supplying four thousand of his own cavalrymen and choosing his son Mircea to spearhead the assault. An angry Sultan Murad retaliates by torturing Dracula and Radu in his dungeon.

1447

Bitter over the previous crusade's failure, and nursing a grudge against Dracula's family, John Hunyadi slaughters the Dragon, his wife Cneajna, and his son Mircea. Vladislav II, one of the Dragon's distant relations, briefly sits on the Walachian throne.

1448

With the backing of Sultan Murad, Dracula takes the throne as prince of Walachia, deposing Vladislav II. His first term as prince is very brief. In November, Hunyadi reinstalls Vladislav II as prince of Walachia. Dracula flees.

1448–1451

Protected by his Uncle Bogdan, Dracula spends three years in intense religious study in Moldavia, alongside his cousin Prince Stephen.

1451

Bogdan is assassinated. Dracula forms an alliance with John Hunyadi, who serves as his military educator and political mentor.

1456

Dracula and Hunyadi lead a massive campaign against the Turks. They also drive Vladislav's men out of Walachia. Dracula retakes the Walachian throne and earns the nickname Vlad the Impaler.

1459

Pope Pius II launches a crusade against the Turks and calls on various European rulers to help him. Dracula is the only ruler who instantly answers the call, which earns him the Vatican's support.

1462

In autumn of this year, the Turkish armies of Sultan Mehmed II lay siege to the Walachian city of Targoviste, where Dracula's palace is located. Thus ends Dracula's second term as prince. It is believed that this is when Dracula's first wife dies. Dracula's brother (and nemesis) Radu the Handsome takes the throne.

1462–1466

The first phase of Dracula's Hungarian exile. At the Hungarian king Matthias's palace in Visegrad, Dracula is held captive at Solomon's Tower.

1466

Dracula ends his stay at Solomon's Tower by converting to Roman Catholicism and marrying into the Hungarian royal family. However, he is still exiled from his beloved Walachia.

1475

Dracula enters into an alliance with King Matthias of Hungary and Stephen the Great of Moldavia.

1476

Dracula reclaims power. This is his third and final term as prince. In December, Dracula is killed under mysterious circumstances.

1897

Irish author Bram Stoker writes the novel *Dracula*.

1931

The Universal Pictures movie *Dracula*, based on Stoker's novel, is released. The film, and actor Bela Lugosi's portrayal of Count Dracula, sets the stage for filmic depictions of vampires for decades to come.

1975

The documentary *In Search of Dracula* is released.

2009

The development of a film chronicling the life of Vlad the Impaler is announced. The movie, to be called *Vlad*, will be produced by Summit Entertainment, the company behind the Twilight series of films.

annals A chronological history.

aristocracy People of the highest social order in a society, or the nobility.

boyar A wealthy landowner.

campaign A series of movements, or military actions, advancing a particular principle or cause.

crusade A vigorous and dedicated action or movement undertaken on behalf of a religious cause.

domnul A prince.

ecclesiastical Of or relating to the church, especially as an organized religious institution.

exile Forced removal from one's native country.

Holy Roman Empire A loosely federated empire that existed in western and central Europe.

impalement A form of execution that involved piercing the condemned person with a sharp stake.

pope Ecclesiastical title for the bishop of Rome; head of the Roman Catholic Church.

progeny One's children or offspring.

testimony A firsthand authentication or declaration of a fact.

vampire The reanimated corpse of a dead person, believed to emerge from the grave at night and drink the blood of the living.

voivode A warrior prince.

Museum of the Moving Image

35 Avenue at 37 Street

Astoria, NY 11106

(718) 784-0077

Web site: http://www.movingimage.us

This museum boasts a large collection of horror movie memorabilia, in addition to artifacts from various other film genres.

Romanian Folk Art Museum

1606 Spruce Street

Philadelphia, PA 19103

(215) 732-6780

Web site: http://www.romanianculture.us

Established in 1983, the Romanian Folk Art Museum boasts a large collection of folkloric artifacts. The museum is dedicated to teaching visitors about Romanian culture.

Romanian National Tourist Office

355 Lexington Avenue, 8th Floor

New York, NY 10017

(212) 545-8484

Web site: http://www.romaniatourism.com

Representing all aspects of Romania's travel industry, the Romanian National Tourist Office was founded in 1968.

Transylvanian Society of Dracula

Canadian Chapter, TSD

2309-397 Front Street West

Toronto, ON M5V 3S1

Canada

Web site: http://blooferland.com/tsd.html

This nonprofit organization is dedicated to the study of both the fictional Count Dracula and Vlad the Impaler. There are also chapters of the Transylvanian Society of Dracula throughout Romania and the rest of Europe.

WEB SITES

Due to the changing nature of Internet links, Rosen Publishing has developed an online list of Web sites related to the subject of this book. This site is updated regularly. Please use this link to access the list:

http://www.rosenlinks.com/vamp/vlad

Augustyn, Michael. *Vlad Dracula: The Dragon Prince*. Bloomington, IN: iUniverse, Inc., 2004.

Bartlett, Wayne, and Flavia Idriceanu. *Legends of Blood: The Vampire in History and Myth*. Westport, CT: Praeger, 2006.

Belford, Barbara. *Bram Stoker and the Man Who Was Dracula*. Cambridge, MA: Da Capo Press, 2002.

Beresford, Matthew. *From Demons to Dracula: The Creation of the Modern Vampire Myth*. London, England: Reaktion Books, 2009.

Goldberg, Enid A., and Norman Itzkowitz. *Vlad the Impaler: The Real Count Dracula*. Danbury, CT: Children's Press, 2007.

Humphries, C. C. *Vlad: The Last Confession*. London, England: Orion Publishing Group, Ltd., 2009.

Jacobson, Sid, and Ernie Colon. *Vlad the Impaler: The Man Who Was Dracula*. New York, NY: Hudson Street Press, 2009.

Karg, Barb, Arjean Spaite, and Rick Sutherland. *The Everything Vampire Book: From Vlad the Impaler to the Vampire Lestat—A History of Vampires in Literature, Film, and Legend*. Avon, MA: Adams Media, 2009.

Knox, Barbara, and Stephen F. Brown. *Castle Dracula: Romania's Vampire Home*. New York, NY: Bearport Publishing, 2005.

Kostova, Elizabeth. *The Historian*. Boston, MA: Little, Brown and Company, 2005.

Miller, Elizabeth. *A Dracula Handbook*. Bloomington, IN: Xlibris Corporation, 2005.

Miller, Elizabeth. *Dracula: Sense & Nonsense*. Essex, England: Desert Island Books, 2000.

Murray, Paul. *From the Shadow of Dracula: A Life of Bram Stoker*.
    London, England: Pimlico, 2005.

Stoker, Bram. *Dracula*. New York, NY: Penguin Books, 1979.

Stoker, Dacre, and Ian Holt. *Dracula the Un-Dead*. New York, NY: Dutton
    Publishing, 2009.

Summers, Montague. *Vampires and Vampirism*. Mineola, NY: Dover
    Publications, 2005.

Trow, M. J. *Vlad the Impaler: In Search of the Real Dracula*.
    Gloucestershire, England: The History Press, 2004.

Wright, Dudley. *Vampires and Vampirism: Legends from Around the World*.
    Maple Shade, NJ: Lethe Press, 2001.

Dalby, Richard, ed. *Dracula's Brood*. New York, NY: Dorset Press, 1987.

Fernandez, Jay A., and Borys Kit. "'The Machinist' Writer Boards Dracula Film." *Hollywood Reporter*, February 15, 2010. Retrieved March 7, 2010 (http://www.hollywoodreporter.com/hr/content_display/film/news/e3i4a73f5d7451749a32145290c4ad5d282).

Florescu, Radu R., and Raymond T. McNally. *Dracula: Prince of Many Faces*. Boston, MA: Little, Brown and Company, 1989.

Geringer, Joseph. "Vlad the Impaler." TruTV Crime Library. Retrieved January 18, 2010 (http://www.trutv.com/library/crime/serial_killers/history/vlad/index_1.html).

Marvel. "Marvel Universe: Dracula." Marvel.com. Retrieved March 1, 2010 (http://marvel.com/universe/Dracula).

McNally, Raymond T., and Radu Florescu. *In Search of Dracula*. Boston: Houghton Mifflin Company, 1994.

Price, Vincent, and V. B. Price. *Monsters*. New York, NY: Grosset & Dunlap, 1981.

Stoker, Bram. *Dracula*. New York, NY: Penguin Books, 1979.

INDEX

ABOUT THE AUTHOR

Arie Kaplan is a comedian, *MAD Magazine* writer, and author of the comic book miniseries *Speed Racer: Chronicles of the Racer* for IDW Publishing. His first nonfiction book, *Masters of the Comic Book Universe Revealed!*, was published by Chicago Review Press in 2006. In addition, he's the author of *From Krakow to Krypton: Jews and Comic Books* (Jewish Publication Society), which was named a *Booklist* Editors' Choice: Books for Youth winner for 2009. *From Krakow to Krypton* was also a finalist for the 2008 National Jewish Book Award, the 2009 ALA Sophie Brody Medal, and the 2009 USA Book News National Best Books 2009 Award. Recently, Kaplan wrote the story and dialogue for the video game *House M.D.* for Legacy Interactive. He has also written for MTV, Cartoon Network, and PBS Kids.

PHOTO CREDITS

Cover Imagno/Getty Images; p. 7 © Werner Baum/dpa/Landov; p. 9 © David Snyder/ZUMA Press; p. 10 © SuperStock; pp. 10–11 Michael Ochs Archives/Getty Images; p. 15 Private Collection/The Stapleton Collection/ The Bridgeman Art Library; pp. 18–19 http://en.wikipedia.org/wiki/ John_Hunyadi; p. 21 http://en.wikipedia.org/wiki/Wallachia; p. 25 http:// en.wikipedia.org/wiki/Vladislav_II_of_Wallachia; p. 28 Scala/Art Resource, NY; pp. 29, 44 © Bogdan Cristel/Reuters/Landov; p. 31 akg-images; p. 35 Marsden, Simon (b.1948)/The Marsden Archive, UK/The Bridgeman/ Art Library; p. 37 © Mary Evans/Ronald Grant/Everett Collection; pp. 40–41 uzo19/http://en.wikipedia.org/wiki/File:Visegradsalamontorony.jpg Összefoglaló; pp. 48–49 © Photos 12/Alamy; p. 50 Stephen Shugerman/ Getty Images; interior graphics (bats) adapted from Shutterstock.com.

Designer: Les Kanturek; Photo Researcher Amy Feinberg